Attic Pieces

By

Nicholas Kriefall

For My Father

Contents

III

IV

I

The Farm

The closet in my bedroom is forbidden.
Nasty little things hide within the coats and shoes;
Mom says they're recluse.

The field seems endless as it molds into the valley.
Arrowheads and bits of pottery
Remain safe from the devouring tractor blade.

Our only chick found its way to the water bucket.
We never knew what it truly was.
Only a toothpick cross proves it existed.

The ducks flow down to the pond in white lines.
At least one will be taken by the snappers.
Past the swing set is treacherous ground.

Patches of Japanese beetles scrape in the grass;
Beautiful little monsters.
To go there barefoot would be my end.

Nostalgia

I once asked my friend
When he could remember being happy.
He responded, "Back when I was poor."

A woman in my church
Lost her husband to cancer,
And then her children to a fire a year later.
She still attends worship every Sunday.

There's a patient in the psychiatric ward I work at
Who sits at his window every day
Staring at the same tree.

He said his father lives in the branches.
I wonder what would happen
If someone went out with a rake
And knocked all the leaves down.

The weekend came and I found other concerns.
Now it is wishing
There was a cushion in this booth.

After Hours

Steam rises from sewers and hot puddles.
A pawnshop lies dark.
The word DIAMONDS in neon red
Gives thieves a fine chill as they pass.

A man urinates through a chain link fence.
When he reads the sign "We are watching you,"
He feels welcomed
And smiles for the security camera.

Their pockets are full;
Everyone owns a piece, a minute,
Some type of shiny memorabilia
To keep forever on their key chain.

The addicts and dealers
Flee in packs once the cops arrive.
Sometime before dawn they'll fall asleep
Clawing into each other like pleased cats.

On the interstate, a van with black windows
Sideswipes a pregnant woman in her car.
When the driver motions her to pull over,
She speeds past into a different lane.

Contrail

The farther ones —
Slivers of light
Fresh upon the sky

Make me think of portals
To other worlds,
Opened by the cut of an angel's wing.

Pretend you're a god and hold one
Between your thumb and finger
Like a needle against the sun.

Think of where they're going
And how you touched their lives
So delicately, they will never know.

Birthday

Further than I could count my mother
Said she hoped he hadn't forgotten.
The invitations said surprise
Though he was never surprised.

So many coats were dumped into my arms.
Fur and musk tickled my nose
All the way to the guest room
Where I piled them on the bed.

I watched from a kitchen cupboard
As they readied the cake.
A girl sat crouched in the dark,
Covered mostly by a sash.

When it was time, Mother sent me to get him.
I climbed the stairs to his chamber door
So tall the maid needed a ladder
To remove the cobwebs that gathered at the top.

Before I knocked I peeked inside.
He sat in his big red chair
Drinking brandy as he watched the fire.
He said no one could build a fire like him.

When he knew I was there, he called me in.
Only the fire lit the room,
Changing the heads and paintings on the walls.
I never liked that and kept my eyes low.

He could always tell when it was me, he said.
Then it was, "Look at that fire."
I watched it with him for a long time
Before Mother came and sent me to bed.

The Astronaut

Two weeks after they landed
She awoke one night
And found him floating on his back
In the pool, wearing his parka.

When it got too cold to be outside
He kept to the basement,
Tinkering with unbroken pipes,
Picking at meals in tinfoil.

After he fell asleep,
She'd sneak downstairs
And breathe on the cellar window
To read his diagrams.

He dreamt peacefully,
Though holding him close,
She knew he was somewhere
Beyond her.

Calm Before the Storm

A caterpillar, heavy with its effort,
Covered in beads
Of the faded morning
Can feel the grass
Weigh under the coming rain
And pauses before the bend.

Miles away, a mosquito
Rises from the boot print of a hunter,
Two seconds born
And already despised by the world,
Save for the three hundred
To follow.

Limbo

The broken stop light
Bleeds into the street,
Closed off by tape and sawhorses.
An old man stands before
The children's hospital,
Holding open his skin
Like a crook selling jewelry.

Fireworks

From lawn chairs and blankets,
On the roofs and hoods of automobiles,
They watch the soulless needles rise,
Racing to find heaven before the end.
Young children tremble
Deceived by the flash and trailing thunder.
The remains drift through the sky
Like the skeletons of spiders
Caught in a breeze.
A car alarm sounds from the dealership.
Birds take from trees and steeples.
Lost behind colored smoke
They search the strange storm for rest.
It isn't long before the teens grow bored,
As fathers point out to those on their laps
The smiley faces and hearts, brief constellations.

Open Sea

Out here I'm allowed to believe
Nothing can reach me.
No warning of clouds has found my vessel.
The sea is a dependable stranger
Beneath a sky just as punishing and blue.
Under blankets of shimmering light
Creatures lurk and glide and feast.
None have touched my invisible trap,
Thin as a needle, held by an unknown bulb.
But I couldn't care less.
I'll go into the shade of the hull
And let the sun caress the air.
Waves will come and rock me to sleep,
And I won't dread going back.

Summer Play

Knowing its danger,
They persist to pump the rusted handle
And flee from the wasps
That have long replaced water.

Dragging their legs
They pursue the half-naked figures
Flailing like the sheets on the clothesline.

The boys take safety in the sprinkler jets
As if the wasps know the rules of tag.
Like sparks in a chimney shaft
They vanish as quickly as they came.

The boys watch them circle the spout
For the best moment to enter,
And then young after the old, creep back.

Bookstore

Tidy and diligent, it smells of coffee
And fresh paper if you're bold enough
To stick your nose between the binds.

Armchairs rest in diamonds
Where customers sit across from one another
Afraid to break the bubble.

They take turns raising their eyes,
Inspecting each other's covers and spines.
Danish is sold on Saturdays;

There's no competition for church.
Relatives shop for birthdays,
Professors hunt for poetry.

The person to tear it down will be a new kind of wretch,
Replacing it with a gas station or parking lot
Or a club where the women keep their underwear on.

Medic

He takes a moment,
looking at the dry blood
on his hand
as he rests on a cedar stump
eating the apple
the general gave him
for saving his leg.

The Affair of the Fallen Cow

In a field barely known to anyone,
Two men walk over the frozen soil
To dispose of a cow that had fallen into the trench.

They step carefully around broken corn stalks,
Ankle-high among the furrows caked with snow.

The one that follows trips and is caught by his friend.
When they continue walking, he can smell her perfume.

He wonders what she'll be wearing when she visits him,
What she'll cook with the steaks he left thawing in the
kitchen,
How long they can keep it up before his friend finds out.

His friend is strong—he could feel it in his grip.
He looks at the hill to the east where the herd used to graze,
And thinks briefly about the cow they left behind.

Behind them a train passes, hissing faintly
From the track cutting through the mountains.
She noticed his hands are rough in the cold;

He shoves them in his pockets as they near a thicket of trees.
He worries about the day she might confess,

And wonders if his friend will lose the field;
But mostly he wonders what she will be wearing tonight.
To their right he watches as two crows pick at a dead hawk.

II

New Year's Eve

The street is visible through the window
In front of the bar.
He watches them pass, the girls and boys,
Not men or women like the couple
In the booth beside him.
He can see their time together by the way
The man pours champagne for his wife.
On the sidewalk a girl spits;
It is the night for anything.

One man will swear off alcohol
When the clock strikes twelve.
Across the room they're not so lucky.
A whisper passes about the man
With a purple drink.
Lovers break the kissing rule early.
The girl in zebra stripes and pearls
Makes them wait in line to buy her drinks;
Mr. Right has yet to look up.
A sports jacket and jewelry hide his bankruptcy.

Phone calls will commence,
Begging for a second chance;
Forgiveness is just a few minutes away.
The limo driver can picture them waiting—
Standing on the couch in their pajamas,
Watching the rain on the street
While the babysitter gets stoned with her boyfriend.
The two he drives haven't the decency
To turn up the window before they get started.

The bum holds his palms over a barrel
Of flaming trash as if he's looking for his child
Growing in its mother's stomach.
He can see them all as they leave,
Stumbling into the night.
A young couple clicks across the cobblestone.

He watches them along the riverfront
Until they disappear.
Midnight and a few twinkling lights.
All that returns is a stray cat.

Sawdust

The smell of sawdust reminds him of his father—
Now an old man fading in a hospital bed,
Perfumed with disinfectant.

Thinking of times he was called to the garage to observe,
He fits a board beneath the blade
And considers the worn teeth.

His eyes move over the cans of varnish,
Yellow labeled and titled by unfamiliar colors.
Tempted to pry one open, instead he turns away
And pulls the length of rope to close the door.

Gravedigger

Resting against the shovel stick,
He wipes his forehead with a handkerchief
And wonders what would happen
If everyone disappeared
And time continued without them.

He wonders how long it would take
For the empty graves to fill with rain,
Or the grass to succumb to weeds.
A robin moves to one of the headstones
And chirps as though it is reading the engravings.

On brighter days, when the sun
Beats down on the back of his neck and arms,
He hopes for the shade that comes before a storm.
Preferring to work under dismal weather
Makes him feel how he believes the mourners feel.

It should be hard to feel lonely, he thinks,
When he stands beneath the sun and trees,
Shoveling dirt onto boxes filled with people who were loved.
He knows he should be considerate every time,
But lost the desire long ago.

He knows it would be the same
Were the people below him in his place.
For a moment he looks up
With a hand over his eyes
To watch a cloud move closer to the sun.

Tapestry

Coy and dignified in an antique room
With furniture and plants,
Vases filled with peacock feathers.
A woman in a large dress
Bends to one of the men
With a delighted look on her face
As he whispers about skinning her a fox.
The second man kneels behind her
To fetch something from under the liquor cabinet,
But for the moment, gazes at her naked calf.
All three look as though they've sampled
More than once from the brandy bottle.
Behind them a suit of armor
Rests on armored horseback.
The boy smiles at his first chance of erotica
Stitched innocently into the horse's breastplate,
Like the dome lid to adolescence
He waits so patiently to be lifted.

Moth Wings

An exquisite terror on one side
Wasn't enough this time.
Had he been smaller,
The boys might never have seen him.

I too was drawn by his size.
I touched the face as soft as I could,
Piercing water without forming a ripple.
Even then I regret taking some of him with me.

I wonder why they felt they had to destroy him.
Had he chosen a different spot to rest,
Above a light fixture or crevice
Where he could have waited for dark.

If only I had been there;
I doubt they would have gone around me.
If only they had chosen a different path home.
If only I had raised them.

On The Beach

There is a large and ugly fish,
Flat and gray, missing its eyes.
Flies swarm around it
And explore every opening
Like miners to a diamond bed.
Its smell beneath the sun is unbearable.
My son pokes at it with a stick,
Sending the flies swirling about.
Had it teeth, he would pluck them
And make a necklace to wear.
As for the scales, like old silver dollars,
He already asked if I wanted one,
But I said no.
He pokes one of the hollow sockets,
Not seeming to tire
When the fish doesn't change.
I watch him a long time,
Hoping he never loses interest.

Helicopters

Wooden with soft edges
And Popsicle stick rotor blades,
He carries it high through the playground,
His tongue flickering behind
Twenty-three small teeth.

It's a steady walk to the corner
Where his grandfather parked the car.
The seeds from a maple tree
Break loose and flutter to the ground.

He lets go of the bony hand to catch one,
Then carries it back
Cupped like a living thing.

When he asks about the war
The old man continues walking,
Hands deep inside his pockets.

Sloth

Surrounded by carcasses
Growing back their fur,
Bottles and jars empty
But for the armies of ants
That sample the glazed bottoms.

The same song spins under a needle
Telling the story of a martyr.
Only the sunset lights the room,
Yellow as bruised skin,
Lighting the mangy carpet on fire.

Cutter

Two days from now I would have
Told him his best friend
Would not be coming home,
And he would have learned about death;
But not like this.
She was a good dog.
I stand over her, the rifle heavy in my hand.
The disease can't hurt her anymore.
She lies still, asleep,
Though I can't tell him that now.
He stands in the drive, crying silently,
Home early from his friend's house.
He's never seen me cry before.
It will take time to get back to where we were,
While she helps the tomatoes grow.

The Karmann Ghia

My brother and I snuck off to its hiding place,
Past the old barn.
The white fortress seemed to keep at our right forever.
We took the gravel road that ended in grass.
Insects snapped through the air like our mother's sprinkler.
It rested in the brush, the body paint faded to cream.
Splotches of rust speckled it like leopard skin;
Its insides were coated in dust.
We imagined it could still work:
My brother tugged back and forth on the rubber-handled
stick shift.
I turned the wheel, but it only moved a few inches.
Anything we could break off we pocketed.
Our small hands struggled with the unknown objects.
Buttons and knobs were easily removed
From the air conditioner and radio.
The rusted Volkswagen symbol jutted out of the ignition.
I grabbed as much as I could with tiny fingers,
And with three hard tugs it popped into my hand,
The teeth still clean.
I held it firmly in my palm,
And then placed it in a pocket by itself.

Night Shift

She can't remember when they
Put the Christmas lights
Around the window with a hole

Where the clerk asks for an I.D.
Or when she grew
Accustomed to falling asleep

To the pink glow of the neon sign.
Nights without it are long
And congested with thought.

The dryer is broken:
Her stockings hang crumpled
From the window like snakeskin.

When she puts them on
The hairs on her legs, arms
And neck rise.

On her way out she applies lipstick
In the broken hallway mirror
Like a spider web telling her to stay.

Stocker

The best day he ever had was in autumn
When it rained and everyone felt the year's first chill.
He started by checking the mousetrap
And found five stuck in the glue
Like a taxidermist's failed attempt.
He spent most of the day
Making cups of pig's brains and ears
Since Daryl had called in with the flu.
He was able to keep eleven jerky strips
A day after their expiration.
The cut on his finger
From the wire of a banana crate
Had healed without a scar.
When the tornado sirens went off,
It was his job to round up customers
Into the dairy freezer until it was clear.
Upon checking the store for others
And locking the doors,
He delayed joining the irritable group.
Standing at the lit up windows,
And darkest sky he could remember
At two in the afternoon, watching the wind
Toss bags and leaves from the parking lot,
There was a sense of majesty
When he faced the store, all to himself.

Elegy for the Fishers of Sugar Bay

It was three days after the Fourth, 1981,
When the boats began to come back empty.
Many of the fishermen had been there before,
Giving the younger men a few days of worry
Before they assured them the fish would be back.
After a couple weeks, and no sign of their catch,
Every captain had to admit that something was wrong.

It was a feeling Captain Cooper had experienced before
When his father was off to war.
His mother called him into the foyer one day,
Standing with two men in military uniforms
With their hats held against their stomachs.
Another time after his dog went missing
And he was forced to remove the flyers around town.

The first day of true concern came in August:
When his ship harbored, he couldn't give his men
A decent answer about the missing fish.
Finnegan had to cut him off an hour before close that night,
And Cooper left, stumbling and cursing the sea.

Every boat came in empty the next few weeks.
Weeks turned into months.
Most of the younger men left the bay to work for their
Fathers, leaving the veterans only to wonder.
The crew of the Silver Maiden was last to surrender.
Cooper took her into storms and the thickest fog,
But the sea defeated her every time.

Finnegan's had its share of colorful nights.
Men would come to drink away the problem,
Most with the mindset that it would work

After the right amount of beer and whiskey.
Over the years Finnegan was wise enough to realize

It would not be him to tell them different,
Especially now when they had nothing to lose.

Fights broke out often—enough for poor Finnegan
To abstain from cleaning until the bar was closed.
Broken items were swept away and not replaced.
One of the veterans, harbored permanently from dementia,
Claimed he had seen it all coming.
He rambled in slurs about spotting a red sun
The day before, and when doubted, defended his word
With an empty beer mug slugged across the jaw—
A practice he made too regular.

After more damage than Finnegan could add up
Without a patient sit down,
He closed the bar and moved farther up the island
Until the problem resolved itself.
His words exactly were: "Let the fish decide."
No one predicted his return anytime soon.

~

Cooper ventured into town seldom for groceries.
At night he drank at a shady tavern but kept it to a minimum.
The last any town member saw of him was at the bank,
Watching a teller pour change
As though he was reminded of a late lover.
He closed his account and asked for more than half in coin
And was no longer seen during the day.

He vanished from the town's eyes,
And his home went dark and cold.
Thomas Crane, his first mate, visited several times
With his wife and swore Cooper had gone.
The town asked questions, but never
Searched for answers and kept the talking prominent.
Only one hooker could vouch for Cooper's existence.
Cooper became just a sound to the bay
By those living closest to the lighthouse.

At least once a week they'd hear rifle fire
And a man screaming obscenities, all to the sea.
The sheriff was too late to find anyone
Whenever he looked into it.

As the months continued to pass, the town deteriorated.
A number of the married couples separated.
Some of the men had warning. Those who clung
To the hope that someday the fish would return
Didn't get so much as a note the day before.
Thomas Crane visited Cooper's residence once more
On his way out of state to work for his father-in-law.
The house appeared darker than before.
Crane never left the car before he and his wife
Said one last prayer for the town, and left.

Most of the ships were sold privately
Or reclaimed by banks and the leasing companies.
Homes were mortgaged, and shops themselves
Lost enough business to go under.
Cooper lost the Silver Maiden the Monday after Easter.
As the surviving citizens watched her go,
He was nowhere to be seen.

Rumors floated of his leaving—more of his
Suicide and the talk of how he had done it.
The speculation that rose most frequently
Was that he had walked straight into the sea
To find the fish and lead them back.
No evidence ever proved the theories,
And he became the second most pondered mystery.

Many of the abandoned shops and homes
Were broken into and ransacked, but never
Was a suspect arrested or questioned.
Most of the bay's policemen were transferred
Farther up the island or clear across state,
Leaving only the sheriff and a deputy before they, too,
Ventured on and the town was left lawless.

With the authorities gone, the town fell like Rome.
Electricity was shut off to more than half;
A single generator was kept running for
The few remaining households and one grocery store.

By fall of 1983, the town was abandoned.
Two months later the fire claimed most of it.
No one could verify completely how it started,
But most believed it was lightning.
Frankly, no one was willing to investigate other possibilities.

With the fish still missing, the town was never restored.
White peaks of ash stood among the remains
Like gravestones and decrepit statues.
The wind carried a bitter sting of charred wood
Instead of sea salt and marine meat.
The sea itself lay quiet and gray,
Yearning for the glitter that abandoned it.

Only a few fishermen went back,
And when they saw what they needed to see
They returned, to what would never feel as right.

Firewood

Beyond the trail, nothing moved.
The white pickup truck blended with the trees.
My father showed us how to spot them—
Which ones were too wet and would kill the fire
And those that would keep it going all night.
When it started to snow again
He told us we could finish if we hurried.
My fingers and toes were numb.
He swore I would never lose them.

Back home, he chopped a large pile for me and my brother
To store in the rack below the porch.
The piles always seemed too much for us,
But my brother assured me we could finish before dark.
We filled the yellow wheelbarrow and my arms,
Though I could only carry two pieces at a time.
He let me ride in the wheelbarrow back to the pile.
It was my job to put it away after we were done.

When I climbed the porch stairs,
My father stood at the door.
He smelled like mouthwash and laughed.
His eyes looked as though he had
Gotten too close while making the fire.
My brother's clothes were in a steaming pile by the stove;
He was already in his room, the door closed.
My father called me to his knee,
And told me how scared he was at times.

I'll never forget the way he split trees
As big and round as barrels,
The snow catching in his beard,
And the smell of the stove on his coat.

III

Neighborhood Watch

Only one person ever saw him as he
Rummaged through a dumpster for sneakers.
A sketch was taken, followed by a drug test—

Negative—and the signs were approved.
Gives a hissing laugh when he sees them
In moonlight, or the wake of the sun.

A companion to raccoons and possums,
Their stomachs fill long before his,
Open to recyclables and any dirty secret.

Feet small enough to leave similar tracks,
Eyes that reflect in the bushes
During sleepover drop offs.

The reason crickets stop chirping,
Lights are hung over garages and front doors,
Flyers of lost pets stay up around town.

Last known proof was at the local campsite
Where security found tissues soaked in gasoline
Like the petals left behind from an infatuated girl.

Solace

The apartment shrinks at night,
Shaped by the pale orange glows
Of antique lamps
She prefers to the overheads.
Boris roams from shadow to shadow,
Phantom as the mark
Cutting his pouty face in half.
The catnip in the clay pot
No bigger than a Styrofoam cup
Never stood a chance.
If he was human, she likes to think
He would be a king,
Sitting center at a table covered with food,
Watching women dance
But too lazy to touch them.
Picturing it makes her laugh,
Until she begins to repeat herself.
Fall brings out the best sunsets.
She watches her favorite part
As she sips from her grandmother's tea set
She was told specifically
To save for company.

In The Gutter

Few might pause if they think
To look at its gathering collection:
Lipstick from a croc-skin purse
That spilled during its snatch
In front of the pharmacy;
A piece of glass from the wreck
Only the bridesmaids survived,
Never expecting to
See a deer in those parts;
And a tiny red bead
Like a drop of blood
That froze during its travel
From a skyscraper roof.
No one would guess that it
Broke from a wreath in July
When the Santa Claus,
Out of uniform, had a stroke.
Only a handful of leaves
Have kept the items from the sewers,
Though under a starless sky
There's as much for relief.

Maintenance Man

In a hallway between numbered doors
And tomorrow's newspapers,
He takes his time.

His radio now silent with the hall
Save for the ringing in his ears
Like the hissing pipes.
The age spot on his left wrist
Resembling Massachusetts was scratched again.

He enters the bathroom and rubs his hands,
Allowed to shake knowing
There is no more work to be done.
Hands that survived another close call,
Made for gripping tools.

He can do anything there—
A secret no one reveals.
He could sit back and watch the building fall
And tip his cap to the rubble.
But for now, with toilet paper,
Helps a spider out of the sink.

Paper Airplane

He made it quickly before anyone
Could see the check beside No,
Bigger than needed, in bold, permanent red.

He thought briefly of looking back
To see if she was using a pen
And hadn't switched to a marker for more impression.

He could still smell the ink as he
Sent the note to the wastebasket
With a sour ounce of hope that it would reach.

Cotton Eye

The girl grips her mother's hand
A little tighter in the teller line
When he looks down and smiles.
He used to wear a patch,
But then it was mistrust instead of an apology
Before they covered their children's eyes
As though he had exposed himself.
He once thought about becoming an attorney
On a night when he was drunk
And using it as an advertising stunt.
Nowadays, he thinks perhaps once
He'll tell a mother and child,
If of course they have the time,
About the day his father
Mowed too close to the gravel drive.

October 31st, 1989

The sidewalk crackled with
Leaves and candy wrappers.

I was the Tin Man—
Cardboard box with arms and legs
Getting high on my metal shine.

My funnel puffed no steam;
My paper tube with Styrofoam blade
Could not hack down a mighty tree.

My pillowcase didn't fill,
Not even halfway.

Houses were endless,
It was time I couldn't beat.

~

He remains frozen
At the edge of the woods.

Home for a Funeral

He stops before the hill, unsure about its ice
And the rear-wheel drive of his cherry red sports car.
He steps out to overlook, though he knows it will go as far
As the knowledge he held when they viewed engines with
their father.

The hillside to the right, owned by who knows now,
Is a thick cover of snow, empty of the sled and foot tracks
That had marked it like a treasure map.
Few trips were ever worth the effort
Before the snow caved beneath their weight.

He continues faster than he would like,
Cringing at every rock he can feel through the floor.
Small mounds jut up from the glade
Where they hunted for scorpions cooling under rocks.

At level ground, he stops again;
The house rests too close beyond the tree line.
He wonders what everyone is doing inside.
Miles away his brother rests on his back,
Made-up to someone he won't recognize.

He recalls the times he stayed up all night
Watching horror movies alone in the basement,
Hearing his brother's alarm at dawn
And pretending to be asleep as he passed to go to work.

The Milkmaid

For Mom

Brightly colored in blues
And yellows of the past—
She tilts the pitcher,
Watching the braid of milk
Unravel in the bowl.
Never could she have known
How many eyes
Would view her work.
Or those who would
Stand for hours at a time
Wondering what it was
She carried in her face.

Casino

It's 11:37 pm on a Sunday.
Mom said Dad gave a good sermon
Last night I turned two dollars into 55
On a penny slot machine.

The free coffee and soda is an idea
I would have loved to take credit for.
The men watching from upstairs
Must have all gotten straight A's in high school.

Several signs in town are burnt out.
I wonder how long it takes for a light to be replaced here;
I can't think of anything more depressing
Than an empty casino when the lights are on.

~

At five in the morning about half have gone home.
Old women I would expect to see
Leaving the Baptist church down the road from my parents' house
Are faithful to the slots.

The poker room holds one game,
The older bartender has relieved his co-worker.
The non-smoking sections are far from their title;
It can travel more than ten feet air-borne.

A biker with a gray beard
Works four machines as he inhales a long cigarette
The Korean couple doesn't fight
Like I've witnessed in their store.

The sign above me rotates slowly—
"The Jack Pot Party" it says,
With past winners listed below,
And the blue convertible someone has yet to win.

47

Barn Owl

On his way to the woodpile
He noticed it, large and solemn
Against the blue night.
The head revolved half a cycle
As though its neck had broken
And it learned to adjust.
Looking at him with a ghostly face,
Eyes like symmetrical inkblots
On a Chinese fan where the artist
Rested his pen too long.
And though knowing it to be harmless
The boy stepped back with fear.
Then by choice or an ill sense
It pushed from the branch
Spreading its layers of brilliant knives,
And sailed into the darkness
Where the power lines ran.

Starlight

Past the orange and green curtains of smog,
Colored so pleasantly by the sun as it sinks
Behind us, another star shines
Like the hope of a dying man.
And just as a speck of glitter
That found the master's painting,
You look at it without any care
To how it got there—
Its life silently ticking away,
Every menacing arm
Reaching for the limitless.
By morning it will be gone,
Replaced by a star far more adored
Until you look at the clock
One minute before
Your alarm was set to go off.

Dog Tags

She mailed them from across the country
In a box once used for earrings—
A riddle in the raised print.

He tattooed them on his left shoulder blade
During a long night of whiskey.

They're missing now,
A few foreign dollars in his pocket.

Afraid to call the step-mother
He never wanted to know,

It will be a one-night stand
Who reads the fresh ink
And recalls his father.

The Ferris Wheel

Just as the sun
Peeked through the clouds
After four straight weeks of rain,
He spots it behind the fog
Like a circus ring set ablaze
Moving only
By the nods of the bow
Where the captain
Lifts his hand to no one.

IV

Sixty-five

His white tee shirt hangs loose,
Stained like an ancient document,
The neck hole three sizes bigger
Than it was when first pulled
From a bag with five others.
His skin is hot and red,
Thick as leather and creased—
Wrinkles running off of wrinkles.
His eyes never failed him, nor his hands,
Or the knee he swore eventually would.
He heard sixty-five is considered old,
The time to think about retiring,
To write a finalized will.
The sun still rises and sets as it always has,
Hay continues to grow and he loves the smell.
At night he wonders what will happen
To everything he leaves behind.
He never imagined nights
Would be this terrifying at sixty-five.

Iraq

Innocence exists in the sandbox,
Even when the two dismember their action figures
And melt the pieces.
Some are lucky enough to be buried alive and forgotten.
I've watched my youngest burn the same G.I. Joe three times;
It is obviously loved.

Sticks and fallen leaves are props
For the war against the insects.
The smaller twigs, jail cell bars,
Hold back the giant grasshopper.
I think it's escaped on several occasions,
But is quickly replaced with another.

I'm used to the sharp pop of bottle rockets.
I still see Mary jump every now and then.
They race up to me and give details
Of the only war I'm interested in—
All the insect parts they saw fluttering through the air.
My fascination isn't fake.

Trapped in an Elevator

It is never that long until the batteries have died
And all they can do is guess the wait.
Courtesy will take its cue
And strangers will talk like friends
Returned from rehab clinics.
Lock them in a box where a man with special keys
Is not on the way
And they'll agree to a corner in which to hold each other.

Perhaps it's the dread of such a future
That causes them to smile
When passing each other on the sidewalk.
Or dying in a strange land years later
Where humans have no shame in robbing a body
Before it has stopped breathing.
Show them there is an end and they'll
Forget what it means to kill for sustenance.

And by then I'm sure our cities will have drowned,
Inhabited with monsters
Blindly luring food with the light of glassless lamps.
Above ground, those who were taught such a trick
Will eat each other;
And though it seems a terrible time
They'll still walk side by side
Like children afraid to hold hands.

Burglar

He persuades the lock
And slips into the darkened home.
Each home he knows carries its own scent.
He takes small items,
Hides them in a duffel bag.
Only on his way out is he detected,
His silent steps broken
By the growl of a black cat.
Within the flashlight's reach
The eyes sliver like a torch flame.
After emptying the bag into a simple pile,
He leaves for the next house empty handed.

Television Set

A box just bigger than a toaster
Covered in dust and plastic wood.
Some tube resembling a coffee straw
Takes place of the missing channel knob.
Numbered to 11, less than half
Gave black and white pictures,
Now lost as ghosts behind a gray screen.
Time passed beyond it, coloring the world.
But there were moments he could have sworn
He saw red in a cartoon mustache,
Roses placed over a casket,
The blood-swelled lips of icons.

School Elegy

The bird lies dead on its back,
Legs extended in the air,
Unbroken it seems, except for the eyes
Black and sunk within the tiny skull—
The brain inside no longer fixed
On flight and food and avoiding predators.
Thoughts on touching it,
He remembers his mother warning
How many diseases they carry,
Though something so small and fragile being a threat
Seems as unlikely as the eyes shaping out
Before it flies away with a mere headache.
He feels the same as he does when the car
Passes those with hand-written signs on the road.
Moving on now like his parents seems too cruel.
After the bell, he nudges the bird with his toe,
And walks into a lesser day.

Horse

The howls rise over the hill
Drowning the men's rustle
Through the leaves
And hiss of their breath in the morning cold.

The fugitive races through the woods
Like a bed sheet ghost
Who smashed the neighborhood Jack-o-lanterns,
Resting in the shadows of trees.

In a barn, his lungs no longer struggling,
He stares into tired eyes,
Free, for now, of the shiny pests
That had cluttered them for a drink.

His legs shake, but otherwise
Are unable to move him.
Every part of his body
Quakes for the river,

If not for these glassy stones
Holding something the judge and jurors never had,
Asking him what is next,
Telling him to move along.

Wheat Penny

Stuck forever in cement,
Blue as a damaged eye.

Tool Shed

They run so hard they forget how thick the grass
Can get around their legs.
Skinny legs that resemble naked chicken bones.
Skinny legs that have yet to run out of panic or fear.
I warn them to be careful around sharp edges.
They come back with scrapes and cuts
And blood they find fascinating.
I tell them to watch out for snakes and thorn bushes,
I tell them to mind their clothes.
They return to me with holes and rips
And socks crawling with burs.
Then they enter the house and flip on the television
And show me, without realizing,
That there are greater threats.

The Orphans

Thousands of years ago
They wandered from the cities
Covered in soot left by the storm.

Some developed a tickle in their throats
After sharing licks
From the woman made of salt.

At a rise, the clean boy waited,
Skin the color of rust, but for his hands
Holding a bowl of warm water.

Arms Collection

He could claim that every item told a story,
And it would not be a lie—
Only that the stories were his own.

After each purchase
He held them with certain gain as though he had
Purchased the conquered lives as well,

The smell of brass stained to his hands like rope burns,
Every nick and scratch
As honest as any fleshly scar.

At times, holding them did the only good
When the treatment didn't work
And he stood bald and pale in a mirror.

Staring at himself, a moment would pass,
Bittersweet as the decision
To put an animal out of misery.

Watson and the Shark

Hard to imagine what he was thinking
Lying across the surface
Looking backwards into the gaping mouth of the beast.

The thin rows of teeth over blood red gums
Flared with a brilliance of the morning sun striking the sea.
I reached for his naked body,
But he only reached for Samuel.

I touched his pale skin
And watched his long blonde hair move into the throat.
Samuel lifted the spear, his foot against the bow,
Aiming for the brain that knew only how to swim and eat.

Night

At 110 pounds my wife asks me if she's fat.
I tell her she is and then rest my palms
On her hipbones at night.
During the day I write a novel
That will never be finished.
When I turn in, she is already asleep.
I crawl into bed in the dark.
Somewhere amidst her endless dreaming
She reaches to confirm I'm there.
I hold her for some time,
Smelling the coconut product in her hair.
Someday she will tell me
I ruined her chance at the life she wanted.
She'll never tell me that I woke her.

Acknowledgements

I am deeply grateful to my family for all of their support and encouragement. Thank you to the editors of Enizagam, Barrow Street, The Ampersand Review, Poetry Quarterly and The Spoon River Poetry Review where some of these poems first appeared. A special thanks goes out to Rubie Grayson, Nicole Pomeroy, and the entire Unsolicited Press team, to Kevin Prufer and Wayne Miller for their insight and direction, and to all those who helped inspire along the way.